# ARABIC
# FIRST
# NAMES

**HIPPOCRENE BOOKS**
*New York*

ISBN 0-7818-0688-7

For information, address:
HIPPOCRENE BOOKS, INC.
171 Madison Avenue
New York, NY 10016

Printed in the United States of America.

*A good name is rather to be chosen
than great riches.*
—PROVERBS 22:1

# Contents

Calligraphy of the name Laïla.

# Girls' Names

### Abida
The feminine form of the name Abid,
derived from *abd* 'servant.'

~~~

### Adiba
The feminine form of the name Adib, meaning 'educated.'

~~~

### Adila
The feminine form of the name Adil, meaning 'just.'
Alternative spelling: Adela.

~~~

### Admaa
From *admaa* 'brown-skinned.'

~~~

### Afaf
From *afaf* 'continence' or 'chastity.'

~~~~~~~~~~~~~~~~~~~~~~~~~~~~~~~~~~~~~~~~

### Afaq
From *afaq* 'horizons.'
Alternative spelling: Afak.

~~~

### Afia
From *afia* 'health.'
Alternative spelling: Afiya.

~~~

### Afifa
The feminine form of the name Afif, meaning 'virtuous.'
Famous bearer of the name: Afifa Yusuf Karam,
Lebanese writer (1883–1924).

~~~

### Afkar
From *afkar* 'thoughts.'

~~~

### Afnan
From *afnan* 'branches' or 'twigs.'

~~~

### Afrah
From *afrah*, plural form of *farah*, meaning 'joy.'

~~~

### Agharid
From *agharid* 'twittering' or 'warbling of birds.'

~~~

### Ahlam
From *ahlam* 'dreams.'

## Aïsha
Feminine form of *aïsh* 'living' or 'living well.'
Famous bearer of the name: Aïsha, favorite wife of the
prophet Muhammad (c. 614–678).

∾∾∾

## Alia
The feminine form of the name Ali, meaning 'noble.'
Alternative spelling: Aliya.

∾∾∾

## Alifa
From *alif* 'friendly' or 'companion.'
Famous bearer of the name: Alifa Rifaat,
Egyptian writer (born 1930).

∾∾∾

## Alissa
Latin name of Dido, the legendary founder and queen of
Carthage in Greek mythology.
Alternative spelling: Elissa.

∾∾∾

## Almas
From *almas* 'diamond.'
Variant: Almasa.

∾∾∾

## Amal
From *amal* 'hope.'

∾∾∾

## Amana
From *amana* 'faithfulness' or 'fidelity.'

### Amani
From *amani*, plural form of the noun *umniya* 'wish'
or 'desire.'

∿∿∿

### Amina
The feminine form of the name Amin,
meaning 'trustworthy.'
Variant: Amna.
Famous bearer of the name: Amina al-Saïd,
Egyptian novelist (born 1914).

∿∿∿

### Amira
From *amira* 'princess.'
Famous bearer of the name: Amira Kamel,
Egyptian opera singer (died 1987).

∿∿∿

### Amra
Derived from *amara* 'to live a long time.'

∿∿∿

### Anan
From *anan* 'clouds.'

∿∿∿

### Angham
From *angham*, plural of *naghm*,
meaning 'tunes' or 'melodies.'

∿∿∿

### Aniqa
Derived from *aniq* 'pretty' or 'elegant.'
Alternative spelling: Anika.

## Anisa
The feminine form of the name Anis, meaning 'cheerful.'

〜〜〜

## Ansam
From *ansam*, plural of *nasam*,
meaning 'breath' or 'breath of life.'

〜〜〜

## Aqila
From *aqila* 'spouse' or 'a noble woman.'
Alternative spelling: Akila.

〜〜〜

## Aqmar
From *aqmar* 'lit by the moon.'
Alternative spelling: Akmar.

〜〜〜

## Arifa
The feminine form of the name Arif, meaning 'knowing.'

〜〜〜

## Arusia
From *arusa* 'bride' or 'puppet.'
Alternative spelling: Arousia.
Famous bearer of the name: Arousia Naalouti,
Algerian writer (born 1950).

〜〜〜

## Arwa
From *arwa* 'beautiful.'

〜〜〜

## Aseel
From *aseel* 'smooth.'

### Ashiqa
The feminine form of the name Ashiq, meaning 'passionate lover.'
Alternative spelling: Ashika.

~~~

### Ashraf
From *ashraf* 'very honorable' or 'the most honorable.'

~~~

### Asila
From *asil* 'rooted.'

~~~

### Asma
From *asma*, plural form of the noun *ism* 'name.'
Famous bearer of the name: Asma Dhat al-Nitaqain,
daughter of the fourth caliph Abu Bakr (died 692).

~~~

### Assia
From *assa* 'to console.'
Alternative spelling: Assiya.
Famous bearer of the name: Assia Djebar,
Algerian writer (born 1936).

~~~

### Atifa
The feminine form of the name Atif, meaning 'kind.'

~~~

### Azhar
From *azhar* 'radiant.'

## Aziza

The feminine form of the name Aziz,
meaning 'powerful' or 'dear.'
Variant: Azza.
Famous bearer of the name: Azza al-Maila,
singer and lute player in Medina (7th century).

∾∾∾

## Azma

Derived from *azima* 'firm will.'
Variants: Azmia, Azmiya.

∾∾∾

# B

## Badia
From *badia* 'desert' or *badi* 'apparent, visible.'
Variant: Badawiya.

❧❧❧

## Badra
Derived from *badr* 'full moon.'
Variant: Badur.

❧❧❧

## Bahia
The feminine form of the name Bahi, meaning 'splendid.'
Alternative spelling: Bahiya.

❧❧❧

## Bahija
From *bahij* 'joyous' or 'beautiful.'

❧❧❧

## Bahira
From *bahir* 'beautiful' or 'admirable.'

❧❧❧

## Bahja
From *bahja* 'joy' or 'beauty.'

❧❧❧

## Bahria
Derived from *bahr* 'brilliance.'
Alternative spelling: Bahriya.

❧❧❧

## Bailasan
From *bailasan* 'elder tree.'

### Baligha
The feminine form of the name Baligh, meaning 'mature.'

~~~

### Balqis
The Arabic name of the Queen of Sheba.
Variant: Bilqis.

~~~

### Bana
From *ban* 'ben tree.'

~~~

### Bashasha
From *bashasha* 'smile' or 'happy demeanor.'

~~~

### Bashira
The feminine form of the name Bashir,
meaning 'bearer of good news.'

~~~

### Basma
From *basma* 'smile.'

~~~

### Bassama
The feminine form of the name Bassam, meaning 'smiling.'
Variant: Bassima.

~~~

### Batul
From *batul* 'virgin.'
Alternative spelling: Batoul.

~~~

### Bushra
From *bushra* 'good news.

9

## D

### Dalia
From *dalia* 'dahlia.'
Alternative spelling: Daliya.

∾∾∾

### Dalila
The feminine form of the name Dalil, meaning 'guide.'

∾∾∾

### Daria
From *dari* 'knowing' or 'wise.'

∾∾∾

### Diya
From *diya* 'light.'

∾∾∾

# F

## Fadia
Feminine form of the name Fadi,
meaning 'someone who sacrifices himself to save others.'
Alternative spelling: Fadiya.

∾∾∾

## Fadila
Feminine form of the name Fadil,
meaning 'virtuous' or 'excellent.'
Alternative spelling: Fadela.

∾∾∾

## Fadwa
Derived from *fida* 'self-sacrifice' or 'devotion.'
Famous bearer of the name: Fadwa Tuqan,
Palestinian poet (born 1917).

∾∾∾

## Fahima
Feminine form of the name Fahim,
meaning 'intelligent' or 'judicious.'
Alternative spelling: Fahema.
Variants: Fahmia, Fahmiya.

∾∾∾

## Faïqa
Feminine form of the name Faïq,
meaning 'excellent' or 'superior.'
Alternative spelling: Faïka.

### Fairuz
From *fairuz* 'turquoise.'
Famous bearer of the name: Fairuz,
Lebanese singer (born c. 1933).

~~~

### Faïza
Feminine form of the name Faïz,
meaning 'successful' or 'victorious.'

~~~

### Farah
From *farah*, meaning 'joy.'
Variant: Farha.

~~~

### Farida
From *farida*, 'beautiful pearl' or 'precious stone.'
Famous bearer of the name: Farida Attiyah,
Lebanese writer (1867–1917).

~~~

### Fathia
Feminine form of the name Fathi, meaning 'open-minded.'

~~~

### Fatiha
Feminine form of the name Fatih,
meaning 'conqueror' or 'victor.'

### Fatima
Feminine form of the name Fatim, meaning 'weaned.'
Variants: Fatma, Fatuma.
Famous bearer of the name: Fatima Mernissi,
Moroccan sociologist and writer (born 1940).

∾∾∾

### Fatin
From *fatin* 'seducing' or 'charming.'
Alternative spelling: Faten.
Famous bearer of the name: Fatin Hamama,
Egyptian actress (born 1932).

∾∾∾

### Fawzia
Feminine form of Fawz, meaning 'success' or 'escape.'
Alternative spelling: Fawziya.

∾∾∾

### Firdaws
From *firdaws* 'paradise.'
Alternative spelling: Firdous.

∾∾∾

## G

### Ghada
Derived from *ghayad* 'softness' or 'tenderness.'
Famous bearer of the name: Ghada Samman,
Lebanese writer (born 1942).

### Ghania
From *ghani* 'rich.'
Alternative spelling: Ghaniya.

### Ghazala
From *ghazala* 'gazelle' or 'rising sun.'

# H

## Habiba
Feminine form of the name Habib, meaning 'beloved.'
Variant: Hababa.
Famous bearer of the name: Habiba Msika,
Tunisian singer (1895–1930).

❧❧❧

## Hadia
From *hadiya* 'present' or 'gift.'
Alternative spelling: Hadiya.

❧❧❧

## Hafiza
Feminine form of the name Hafiz,
meaning 'guardian' or 'keeper.'
Alternative spelling: Hafisa.

❧❧❧

## Hajar
From *hajar* 'stone.'
Alternative spelling: Hagar.
Famous bearer of the name: Hagar in the Old Testament,
concubine of Abraham and mother of Ishmael.

❧❧❧

## Hala
From *hala* 'ring around the moon or the sun.'

❧❧❧

## Halima
From *halim* 'gentle' or 'mild.'
Famous bearer of the name: Halima, daughter of the
Ghassanid king al-Harith al-Araj (6th century).

### Hamima
From *hamim* 'close friend.'

~~~

### Hana
From *hana* 'joy' or 'congratulations.'

~~~

### Hanan
From: *hanan* 'tenderness' or 'compassion.'
Famous bearer of the name: Hanan al-Sheikh,
Lebanese writer (born 1945).

~~~

### Hasna
From *hasna* 'beautiful woman' or 'beauty.'

~~~

### Hassana
Feminine form of the name Hassan, meaning 'excellent.'

~~~

### Hawa
The Arabic form of Eva.

~~~

### Hayat
From *hayat* 'life.'

~~~

### Hiba
From *hiba* 'present' or 'gift.'
Alternative spelling: Heba.

### Hind
From *hind* 'India.'
Famous bearer of the name: Hind Nafwal,
Lebanese magazine publisher and editor (c. 1860–1920).

∾∾∾

### Huda
From *hudan* 'right guidance' or 'right way.'
Variant: Hoda.
Famous bearer of the name: Hoda Shaarawi,
Egyptian feminist (1879–1949).

∾∾∾

### Hurriya
From *hurriya* 'liberty.'

∾∾∾

### Husnia
Feminine form of the name Husn, meaning 'beauty.'
Variant: Husniya.

∾∾∾

# I

**Ibtihaj**
From *ibtihaj* 'joy.'

~~~

**Ibtihal**
From *ibtihal* 'supplication' or 'prayer.'

~~~

**Ibtisam**
From *ibtisam* 'smile.'

~~~

**Iftitan**
Derived from *iftatana* 'to be charmed.'

~~~

**Ikhlas**
From *ikhlas* 'sincerity.'

~~~

**Ikram**
From *ikram* 'glorification' or 'exaltation.'

~~~

**Ilham**
From *ilham* 'inspiration.'

~~~

**Ilhan**
From *ilhan*, plural of *lahn*, meaning 'tune' or 'melody.'

## Iman

From *iman* 'faith.'
Famous bearer of the name: Iman Abdulmajid,
Somalian-born fashion model (born 1957).

~~~

## Inaam

From *inaam* 'given by God.'

~~~

## Inas

From *inas* 'friendliness' or 'sociability.'

## Israa

From *israa* 'nocturnal journey.'

~~~

## Intisar

From *intisar* 'victory.'

~~~

## Izdihar

From *izdihar* 'flourishing' or 'bloom.'

~~~

# J

### Jahida
Derived from *jahada* 'to make an effort' or 'to exert oneself.'
Alternative spelling: Jaheda.

∾∾∾

### Jalila
Feminine form of the name Jalil, meaning 'great.'

∾∾∾

### Jamal
From *jamal* 'beauty' or 'grace.'

∾∾∾

### Jamila
From *jamil* 'beautiful.'
Famous bearer of the name: Jamila,
Arab singer in Medina (died c. 720).

∾∾∾

### Janna
From *janna* 'paradise' or 'garden.'
Variant: Jinan.

∾∾∾

### Jawhar
From *jawhara* 'jewel' or 'pearl.'
Variant: Jawhara.

## Jihan

From Persian, meaning 'world.'
Alternative spelling: Jehan.
Famous bearer of the name: Jihan al-Sadat, writer and wife of the Egyptian president Anwar al-Sadat (born 1933).

∾∾∾

## Jumana

From *jumana* 'pearl.'

∾∾∾

### 𝕂

## Kamila
Feminine form of the name Kamil,
meaning 'perfect' or 'complete.'
Variant: Kamilia.

≈≈≈

## Kanza
Derived from *kanz* 'treasure.'
Alternative spelling: Kenza.

≈≈≈

## Karima
Feminine form of the name Karim,
meaning 'noble' or 'generous.'
Alternative spelling: Kerima.

≈≈≈

## Kawkab
From *kawkab* 'star.'

≈≈≈

## Khadija
From *khadīj* 'born prematurely.'
Alternative spelling: Khadidja.
Variant: Didja.
Famous bearer of the name: Khadija,
first wife of the prophet Muhammad.

≈≈≈

## Khaira
From *khair* 'good.'

### Khalida
Feminine form of the name Khalid,
meaning 'everlasting' or 'eternal.'

~~~

### Khalisa
Feminine form of the name Khalis, meaning 'pure.'

~~~

### Khulud
From *khulud* 'eternity.'

~~~

### Khuzama
From *khuzama* 'lavender.'

~~~

# 𝕷

## Labiba
Feminine form of the name Labib, meaning 'intelligent.'
Famous bearer of the name: Labiba Nasif Madi,
Lebanese writer (1880–1947).

∾∾∾

## Laïla
From *laïla* 'night.'
Alternative spelling: Layla, Leila.
Famous bearer of the name: Laïla Baalbaki,
Lebanese writer (born 1934).

∾∾∾

## Lamia
From *lami* 'shining' or 'bright.'
Alternative spelling: Lamiya.
Famous bearer of the name: Lamia Amara,
Iraqi poet (born 1927).

∾∾∾

## Latifa
From *latif* 'kind.'
Famous bearer of the name: Latifa al-Zayyat,
Egyptian writer (born 1924).

∾∾∾

## Lutfia
Feminine form of the name Lutfi, meaning 'friendliness.'
Alternative spelling: Lutfiya.

∾∾∾

# M

### Maamuna
Feminine form of the name Maamun, meaning 'trustworthy.'
Alternative spelling: Maamouna.

### Mabruka
Feminine form of the Name Mabruk, meaning 'blessed.'
Alternative spelling: Mabrouka.

### Madiha
From *madih* 'one who eulogizes.'
Alternative spelling: Madeha.

### Maha
From *maha* 'small mountain trail or hollow full of water.'

### Mahasin
From *mahasin* 'charms' or 'good qualities.'
Alternative spelling: Mahasen.

### Mahbuba
Feminine form of the name Mahbub,
meaning 'beloved' or 'liked.'
Alternative spelling: Mahbouba.

### Mahdia
Feminine form of the name Mahdi, meaning 'rightly guided.'
Alternative spelling: Mahdiya.

## Mahfuza

Feminine form of the name Mahfuz, meaning 'guarded.'
Alternative spelling: Mahfouza.

∾∾∾

## Mahira

Feminine form of the name Mahir, meaning 'skillful.'
Alternative spelling: Mahera.

∾∾∾

## Mahmuda

Feminine form of the name Mahmud,
meaning 'praised' or 'praiseworthy.'

∾∾∾

## Maïmana

From *maïmana* 'fortune.'

∾∾∾

## Maïmuna

Feminine form of the name Maïmun, meaning 'fortunate.'
Alternative spellings: Maïmouna, Mimouna.

∾∾∾

## Maisara

From *maisara* 'ease' or 'wealth.'

∾∾∾

## Maïsun

Derived from *masa* 'to walk with a lofty, proud, swinging gait.'
Alternative spelling: Maïsoun.
Famous bearer of the name: Maïsun, wife of the caliph
Muawiya and mother of the caliph Yazid (7th century).

## Majdia

Feminine form of the name Majdi, meaning 'glorious.'
Alternative spelling: Majdiya.

## Majida

Feminine form of the name Majid,
meaning 'noble' or 'glorious.'
Famous bearer of the name: Majida al-Roumi,
Lebanese singer (born 1956).

## Malak

From *malak* 'angel.'
Famous bearer of the name: Malak Abdulaziz,
Egyptian poet (born 1921).

## Malda

Derived from *malida* 'to be delicate.'

## Maliha

Derived from *maliha* 'to be beautiful.'

## Malika

From *malika* 'queen.'
Variant: Mulaika.

## Mamduha

Feminine form of the name Mamduh, meaning 'praised.'

### Manal
From *manal* 'achievement.'

∾∾∾

### Mansura
Feminine form of the name Mansur,
meaning 'aided by God' or 'victorious.'
Alternative spelling: Mansoura.

∾∾∾

### Maqbula
Feminine form of the name Maqbul, meaning 'accepted.'

∾∾∾

### Marjan
From *marjan* 'corals' or 'small pearls.'
Variant: Marjana.

∾∾∾

### Maryam
The Arabic form of Mary.
Alternative spellings: Miriam, Meriam, Mariem.
Famous bearer of the name: Maryam bint Abi Yaqub,
Andalusian poet (11th century).

∾∾∾

### Marzuka
Feminine form of the name Marzuk,
meaning 'blessed with worldly goods.'

∾∾∾

### Masuda
Feminine form of the name Masud,
meaning 'favored by luck' or 'lucky.'
Alternative spelling: Masouda.

## Mawhuba
Feminine form of the name Mawhub,
meaning 'talented' or 'gifted.'

༄༅༅

## Mawluda
Feminine form of the name Mawlud, meaning 'newly-born.'

༄༅༅

## Mayy
From Persian origin, meaning 'wine.'
Famous bearer of the name: Mayy Ziyade, Lebanese writer
(1886–1941).

༄༅༅

## Mirnan
From *mirnan* 'ring of a voice' or 'jingle.'

༄༅༅

## Mufida
Feminine form of the name Mufid, meaning 'beneficial.'
Alternative spelling: Moufida.

༄༅༅

## Muhsina
Feminine form of the name Muhsin, meaning 'benefactor.'
Alternative spelling: Mohsina.

༄༅༅

## Mukhlisa
Feminine form of Mukhlis, meaning 'sincere.'

༄༅༅

## Mukhtara
Feminine form of the name Mukhtar,
meaning 'preferred' or 'chosen by God.'
Alternative spelling: Mokhtara.

## Mumina
Feminine form of Mumin, meaning 'believer.'

ᔆᔆᔆ

## Muna
From *muna* 'wishes' or 'desires.'
Alternative spelling: Mona.

ᔆᔆᔆ

## Munia
From *munia* 'wish' or 'desire.'
Alternative spelling: Muniya.

ᔆᔆᔆ

## Muniba
Feminine form of the name Munib, meaning 'repentant.'

ᔆᔆᔆ

## Munifa
Feminine form of the name Munif,
meaning 'sublime' or 'excellent.'

ᔆᔆᔆ

## Munira
Feminine form of the name Munir,
meaning 'luminous' or 'shining.'
Alternative spelling: Mounira.

ᔆᔆᔆ

## Munjia
Derived from *naja* 'to escape.'
Alternative spelling: Monjiya.

ᔆᔆᔆ

## Muntasira
Feminine form of the name Muntasir,
meaning 'victorious' or 'conquering.'

### Murida
Feminine form of the name Murid,
meaning 'disciple' or novice.'

∾∾∾

### Musadaqqa
Feminine form of the name Musaddak,
meaning 'sincere' or trustworthy.'

∾∾∾

### Mutasima
Feminine form of the name Mutasim,
meaning 'someone who takes refuge.'

∾∾∾

### Mutawakkila
Feminine form of the name Mutawakkil,
meaning 'someone who trusts in another person.'

∾∾∾

### Muzaffara
Feminine form of Muzaffar, meaning 'victorious.'

∾∾∾

## Nabiha
Feminine form of the name Nabih,
meaning 'noble' or 'excellent.'

~~~

## Nabila
Feminine form of the name Nabil,
meaning 'noble' or 'aristocratic.'

~~~

## Nada
From *nada* 'moisture' or 'dew.'

~~~

## Nadia
Derived from *nadiya* 'to have dew on the surface.'
Famous bearer of the name: Nadia Boulanger, French
teacher, composer and conductor (1887–1979).

~~~

## Nadima
Feminine form of the name Nadim,
meaning 'associate' or 'friend.'

~~~

## Nadira
Feminine form of the name Nadir,
meaning 'rare' or 'precious.'

~~~

## Nadra
From *nadra* 'rarity.'
Variant: Nudra.

### Nafisa
Feminine form of the name Nafis,
meaning 'valuable' or 'precious.'
Variant: Nufaisa.

∾∾∾

### Nahid
From *nahid* 'in the bloom of youth.'
Variant: Nahida.

∾∾∾

### Naïla
Derived from *nala* 'to give.'

∾∾∾

### Naïma
Feminine form of the name Naïm,
meaning 'contended' or 'tranquil.'

∾∾∾

### Najia
Feminine form of the name Naji, meaning 'close friend.'
Alternative spelling: Najiya.

∾∾∾

### Najiba
Feminine form of the name Najib, meaning 'noble.'

∾∾∾

### Najla
From *najla* 'having big eyes.'
Alternative spelling: Nejla.
Famous bearer of the name: Najla Abu al-Luma,
Lebanese writer (1895–1967).

### Najm
From *najm* 'star.'
Variant: Najma.

∾∾∾

### Naqia
From *naqi* 'pure.'
Alternative spelling: Naqiya.

∾∾∾

### Nariman
From Persian, meaning 'beauty of body.'

∾∾∾

### Narjis
From *narjis* 'daffodil.'
Alternative spellings: Narjes.
Variant: Nirjis.

∾∾∾

### Nashita
Feminine form of Nashit, meaning 'active' or 'energetic.'

∾∾∾

### Nasira
Feminine form of Nasir, meaning 'helper.'

∾∾∾

### Nasria
Derived from *nasr* 'help' or victory.'
Alternative spelling: Nasriya.

∾∾∾

### Nawal
From *nawal* 'gift' or 'favor.'
Famous bearer of the name: Nawal al-Saadawi,
Egyptian writer (born 1931).

## Nawfar
From *nawfar* 'water-lily.'

~~~

## Nawra
From *nawra* 'blossom.'

~~~

## Nayyira
Feminine form of the name Nayyir,
meaning 'shining' or 'bright.'

~~~

## Naziha
From *nazih* 'pure' or 'untouched.'

~~~

## Nazik
Derived from *naizak* 'shooting star' or 'meteor.'
Famous bearer of the name: Nazik al-Malaïka,
Iraqi poet and critic (born 1923).

~~~

## Nazima
Feminine form of the name Nazim, meaning 'poet.'

~~~

## Nisrin
From *nisrin* 'jonquil.'
Variants: Nisrina, Nasreen.

~~~

## Nur
From *nur* 'light.'
Alternative spelling: Nour.

~~~

## Q

### Qamar
From *qamar* 'moon.'
Famous bearer of the name: Qamar al-Kilani,
Syrian writer (born 1932).

〜〜〜

### Qamra
From *qamra* 'moonlit.'

〜〜〜

### Qasima
Derived from *qasam*, meaning 'beauty' or 'elegance.'
Alternative spelling: Kasima.

〜〜〜

# ℛ

## Rabia
Derived from *rabi* 'spring.'
Alternative spelling: Rabiya.
Famous bearer of the name: Rabiya al-Adawiya,
Arab female saint (c. 714–801).

ᘓᘓᘓ

## Radia
From *radi* 'satisfied.'
Alternative spelling: Radiya.

ᘓᘓᘓ

## Rafida
From *rafid* 'someone who assists.'
Alternative spelling: Rafeda.

ᘓᘓᘓ

## Rafiqa
Feminine form of the name Rafiq, meaning 'companion.'
Alternative spelling: Rafika.

ᘓᘓᘓ

## Rahima
Feminine form of the name Rahim, meaning 'compassionate.'

ᘓᘓᘓ

## Rahma
From *rahma* 'compassion.'

ᘓᘓᘓ

## Raïda
Feminine form of Raïd, meaning 'pioneer.'

### Raja
From *raja* 'hope.'

~~~

### Rajia
From *raji* 'hoping.'
Alternative spelling: Rajiya.

~~~

### Rajwa
Derived from *raja* 'to hope.'
Alternative spelling: Rajoua.

~~~

### Rakina
From *rakin* 'reliable' or 'firm.'

~~~

### Ramzia
Feminine form of the name Ramzi, meaning 'symbolic.'
Alternative spelling: Ramziya.

~~~

### Raoufa
Feminine form of the name Raouf, meaning 'compassionate.'

~~~

### Rashida
Feminine form of the name Rashid,
meaning 'follower of the right way.'

~~~

### Rashiqa
From *rashiq* 'elegant' or 'svelte.'
Alternative spelling: Rashika.

## Rawda
From *rawda* 'garden.'

~~~

## Rayan
From *rayyan* 'beautiful' or 'exuberant.'

~~~

## Raziqa
From *raziq* 'granting' or 'bestowing.'

~~~

## Rim
From *rim* 'white antelope.'
Alternative spellings: Rym, Reem.
Variant: Rima.

~~~

## Ruhia
From *ruhia* 'spirituality.'
Alternative spelling: Ruhiya.

~~~

## Rushdia
Derived from *rushd* 'rectitude' or 'maturity.'
Alternative spelling: Rushdiya.

~~~

## Ruwaida
From *ruwaidan* 'slowly' or 'gently.'

~~~

### Saadia
Derived from *saad* 'luck' or 'success.'
Alternative spellings: Saadiya, Sadia, Sadiya.

≈≈≈

### Sabah
From *sabah* 'morning.'

≈≈≈

### Sabiha
From *sabih* 'pretty' or 'beautiful.'

≈≈≈

### Sabira
Feminine form of the name Sabir, meaning 'patient.'

≈≈≈

### Sabria
Derived from *sabr*, meaning 'patience.'
Alternative spelling: Sabriya.

≈≈≈

### Sadida
Feminine form of the name Sadid, meaning 'right' or 'true.'
Variant: Sidida.

≈≈≈

### Sadiqa
From *sadika* 'friend.'
Alternative spellings: Sadiqa, Sadeeka.
Variant: Sidiqa.

### Safa
From *safa* 'serenity of life' or 'pleasure.'

∾∾∾

### Safia
From *safia* 'pure' or 'serene.'
Alternative spelling: Safiya.

∾∾∾

### Sahar
From *sahar* 'early daybreak.'
Famous bearer of the name: Sahar Khalifa,
Palestinian author (born 1941).

∾∾∾

### Sajaya
From *sajaya* 'traits of character.'

∾∾∾

### Saïda
From *saïda* 'happy.'

∾∾∾

### Sajia
From *sajia* 'natural disposition.'
Alternative spelling: Sajiya.

∾∾∾

### Sajida
Feminine form of Sajid, meaning 'worshipper.'

∾∾∾

### Sajwa
From *sajw* 'quiet.'

## Sakina
From *sakina* 'divine silence.'
Alternative spelling: Sakeena.
Variant: Sukaina.

~~~

## Saliha
Feminine form of the name Salih, meaning 'good' or 'just.'
Variant: Saleha.
Famous bearer of the name: Saliha,
Tunisian singer of Maalouf music (1914–1958).

~~~

## Salima
Feminine form of the name Salim, meaning 'faultless.'
Alternative spellings: Saleema.
Variants: Salma, Selma.
Famous bearer of the name: Salma Hayek,
Mexican actress of Lebanese origin (born 1968).

~~~

## Salwa
From *salwa* 'quail' or 'consolation.'
Famous bearer of the name: Salwa al-Banna,
Palestinian writer (born 1948).

~~~

## Sama
From *sama* 'heaven.'

~~~

## Samah
From *samah* 'kindness' or 'grace.'

## Samar

From *samar* 'nightly conversation.'
Famous bearer of the name: Samar Attar,
Syrian writer (born 1940).

❧❧❧

## Samia

Feminine form of the name Sami, meaning 'high' or 'noble.'
Alternative spelling: Samiya.

❧❧❧

## Samiha

Feminine form of the name Samih,
meaning 'lenient' or 'tolerant.'

❧❧❧

## Samira

Feminine form of the name Samir,
meaning 'entertainer' or 'narrator.'

❧❧❧

## Sana

From *sana* 'sublimity' or 'high rank.'

❧❧❧

## Sania

From *sania* 'high' or 'noble.'
Alternative spelling: Saniya.

❧❧❧

## Sawsan

From *sawsan* 'lily.'
Variant: Sawsana.

### Sayida
From *sayida* 'lady' or 'mistress.'

~~~

### Shadia
Feminine form of the name Shadi, meaning 'educated.'
Alternative spelling: Shadya.

~~~

### Shadhlia
Derived from Abu al-Hasan al-Shadhili,
founder of the Shadhilia mystic order.
Alternative spelling: Shadliya.

~~~

### Shafiqa
From *shafiqa* 'compassionate.'
Alternative spelling: Shafika.

~~~

### Shahida
Feminine form of the name Shahid,
meaning 'witness' or 'martyr.'
Alternative spelling: Shaheeda.

~~~

### Shakira
Feminine form of the name Shakir, meaning 'thankful.'
Variant: Shakura.

~~~

### Shams
From *shams* 'sun.'

### Sharifa
Feminine form of the name Sharif, meaning 'honorable'

❦❦❦

### Shawq
From *shawq* 'longing' or 'desire.'
Variant: Shawqia.

❦❦❦

### Shirin
From Persian, meaning 'pretty' or 'nice.'

❦❦❦

### Sidqia
Derived from *sidq*, meaning 'truth' or 'sincerity.'
Alternative spelling: Sidkiya.

❦❦❦

### Siham
From *siham* 'arrows.'

❦❦❦

### Suad
Derived from *saad* 'luck.'
Alternative spelling: Souad.

❦❦❦

### Suha
From *suha*, a small planet in Ursa Minor or Ursa Major.

❦❦❦

### Suhaila
From *suhail* 'canopus, a star of the first magnitude
in the constellation Carina.'
Variant: Souhila.

### Suhair

Diminutive of *sahar*, meaning 'watchfulness' or 'vigilance.'
Famous bearer of the name: Suhair al-Qalamawi,
Egyptian writer and critic (born 1911).

꩜꩜꩜

### Sumia

Derived from *sumuw* 'sublimity.'
Alternative spellings: Sumiya, Soumiya.

꩜꩜꩜

### Surur

From *surur* 'joy.'

꩜꩜꩜

## T

### Taghrid
From *taghrid* 'singing' or 'twittering, warbling.'

~~~

### Tahani
From *tahani* 'congratulations' or 'felicitations.'

~~~

### Tahira
From *tahir* 'pure' or 'innocent.'

~~~

### Tala
From *tala* 'small palm tree.'

~~~

### Talida
From *talida* 'inherited, time-honored property.'

~~~

### Tamima
Derived from *tamma* 'to be complete.'

~~~

### Taqia
From *taqi* 'devout.'
Alternative spelling: Taqiya.

~~~

### Tawfiqa
Feminine form of the name Tawfiq,
meaning 'success' or 'prosperity.'

## Thuraya

From *al-thuraya* 'the Pleiades,' a conspicuous cluster of stars in the constellation Taurus.'
Alternative spellings: Suraya, Soraya.

❧❧❧

## Tuhfa

From *tuhfa* 'unique work of art.'

❧❧❧

# 𝔘

## Ulfa

From *ulfa* 'love' or 'harmony.'
Variant: Olfa.
Famous bearers of the name: Ulfa Idelbi,
Syrian writer (born 1912).

❧❧❧

# 𝔚

## Wadia
Feminine form of the name Wadi, meaning 'gentle.'
Alternative spelling: Wadiya.

∾∾∾

## Wadida
Feminine form of the name Wadid, meaning 'affectionate.'
Variant: Waduda.

∾∾∾

## Wafa
From *wafa* 'fidelity.'

∾∾∾

## Wafia
From *wafia* 'faithful' or 'loyal.'
Alternative spelling: Wafiya.

∾∾∾

## Wafiqa
Derived from *wafaqa* 'to agree.'
Alternative spelling: Wafika.

∾∾∾

## Wahiba
Feminine form of the name Wahib, meaning 'one who gives.'

∾∾∾

## Wahida
Feminine form of the name Wahid, meaning 'unique.'

## Wajdia

Derived from *wajd* 'passion.'
Alternative spelling: Wajdiya.

~~~

## Wajida

Feminine form of the name Wajid, meaning 'enamored.'

~~~

## Walia

From *walia* 'mistress.'
Alternative spelling: Waliya.

~~~

## Walida

Feminine form of the name Walid, meaning 'newborn.'

~~~

## Warda

From *warda* 'rose.'
Variants: Wardia, Wardiya.
Famous bearer of the name: Warda,
Algerian singer (born 1940).

~~~

## Wasama

From *wasama* 'grace.'

~~~

## Wasila

Feminine form of the name Wasil,
meaning 'inseparable friend.'

## Wasima

Feminine form of the name Wasim, meaning 'attractive.'
Variant: Wasma.

≈≈≈

## Widad

From *widad* 'love' or 'friendship.'
Famous bearer of the name: Widad Sakakini,
Lebanese short story writer (1913–1991).

≈≈≈

## Wijdan

From *wijdan* 'soul' or 'strength of soul.'

≈≈≈

♈

## Yamama
From *yamama* 'wild pigeon.'

~~~

## Yamina
Derived from *yamana* 'to be happy.'

~~~

## Yasmin
From *yasmin* 'jasmine.'
Variant: Yasmina.

~~~

## Yumna
Derived from *yumn* 'success' or 'luck.'
Variants: Yumnia, Yumniya.

~~~

## Yusra
From *yusr* 'wealth.'
Alternative spelling: Yousra.
Variants: Yusria, Yusriya.

~~~

## Yaquta
From *yaqut* 'precious stone.'

~~~

# Z

**Zada**
Derived from *zada* 'to grow.'

**Zafira**
Feminine form of the name Zafir, meaning 'victorious.'

**Zahia**
From *zahia* 'beautiful.'
Alternative spelling: Zahiya.

**Zahida**
Feminine form of the name Zahid, meaning 'ascetic.'
Alternative spelling: Zaheda.

**Zahira**
Feminine form of the name Zahir, meaning 'radiant.'
Alternative spelling: Zahera.

**Zahra**
From *zahra* 'flower' or 'blossom.'

**Zaïna**
Feminine form of the name Zaïn, meaning 'embellishment.'
Alternative spelling: Zeina.

## Zainab

From *zain ab*, 'meaning adornment of the father.'
Alternative spellings: Zaineb, Zeineb.
Famous bearer of the name: Zainab Fahmi,
Egyptian writer (born 1935).

෧෧෧

## Zakia

Feminine form of the name Zaki,
meaning 'pure' or 'innocent.'
Alternative spelling: Zakiya.

෧෧෧

## Zuhra

From *zuhra* 'beauty.'
Alternative spelling: Zohra.
Variant: Zuhaira.

෧෧෧

## Zuhur

From *zuhur* 'flowers.'
Famous bearer of the name: Zuhur Ali Unisa,
Algerian writer of short stories (born 1936).

෧෧෧

## Zumurrud

From *zumurrud* 'emerald.'
Variant: Zumurruda.

Calligraphy of the name Abdullatif.

# Boys' Names

## A

### Abbas
Derived from *abasa* 'to have a
severe expression on the face' or 'to frown.'
Alternative spelling: Abbes.
Variant: Abbasi.
Famous bearers of the name: Abbas Hilmi I,
viceroy of Egypt (1813–1854);
Abbas Mahmud al-Aqqad,
Egyptian journalist, poet and writer (1889–1964).

### Abduh
Derived *abd* 'servant' meaning 'his (God's) servant.'
Alternative spellings: Abdo, Abdou.
Famous bearers of the name: Abdou Diouf,
president of Senegal (born 1935);
Abduh al-Hamuli, Egyptian musician (1845–1901).

## Abdulaziz

From *abd* 'servant' + *al-aziz* 'the powerful'—in Islam one of
the 100 names of God—meaning 'servant of the powerful.'
Famous bearer of the name: Abdulaziz ibn Saud,
king of Saudi Arabia (c. 1880–1953).

## Abdulfattah

From *abd* 'servant' + *al-fattah* 'the one who opens the gate to
well-being and prosperity'—in Islam one of the 100 names of
God—meaning 'servant of the one who opens the gate to
well-being and prosperity.'
Famous bearer of the name: Abdulfattah Abada,
Egyptian writer and historian (born 1928).

## Abdulhafiz

From *abd* 'servant' + *al-hafiz* 'the guardian'—in Islam one of
the 100 names of God—meaning 'servant of the guardian.'
Alternative spelling: Abdulhafid.
Famous bearer of the name: Abdulhafiz,
sultan of Morocco (c. 1875–1937).

## Abdulhakim

From *abd* 'servant' + *al-hakim*, 'the wise'—in Islam one of the
100 names of God—meaning 'servant of the wise.'
Famous bearer of the name: Abdulhakim Amir,
Egyptian nationalist and politician (1913–1967).

## Abdulhalim

From *abd* 'servant' + *al-halim* 'gentle'—in Islam one of the
100 names of God—meaning 'servant of the gentle.'
Famous bearer of the name: Abdulhalim Hafiz,
Egyptian singer (1929–1977).

ოოო

## Abdulhamid

From *abd* 'servant' + *al-hamid* 'the praised'—in Islam one of
the 100 names of God—meaning 'servant of the praised.'
Famous bearer of the name: Abdulhamid I,
Ottoman sultan of Turkey (1725–1989);
Abdulhamid al-Dib, Egyptian poet (1899–1943).

ოოო

## Abdulkarim

From *abd* 'servant' + *al-karim* 'the noble'—in Islam one of the
100 names of God—meaning 'servant of the noble.'
Alternative spelling: Abdelkrim.
Famous bearer of the name: Abdulkarim al-Karmi,
Palestinian poet (1907–1980);
Abdelkrim, leader of the Rif tribes of Morocco (c. 1862–1963).

ოოო

## Abdulkhaliq

From *abd* 'servant' + *al-khaliq*, 'the creator'—in Islam one of
the 100 names of God—meaning 'servant of the creator.'
Alternative spelling: Abdulkhalik.
Famous bearer of the name: Abdulkhaliq ibn Abi Talha,
Yemenite poet (9th century).

## Abdullah
From *abd* 'servant' + *allah* 'God,' meaning 'God's servant.'
Alternative spelling: Abdulla.
Famous bearer of the name: Abdullah,
king of Jordan (1882–1951).

## Abdullatif
From *abd* 'servant' + *al-latif* 'the kind'—in Islam one of the
100 names of God—meaning 'servant of the kind.'
Famous bearer of the name: Abdullatif al-Baghdadi,
Islamic philosopher (1162–1231).

## Abdulmajid
From *abd* 'servant' + *al-majid* 'the glorious'—in Islam one of
the 100 names of God—meaning 'servant of the glorious.'
Famous bearer of the name: Abdulmajid ibn Abdulaziz,
Ottoman sultan of Turkey (1823–1861).

## Abdulmalik
From *abd* 'servant' + *al-malik* 'the king'—in Islam one of the
100 names of God—meaning 'servant of the king.'
Famous bearer of the name: Abdulmalik,
fifth Umayyad caliph (c. 646–705).

## Abdulmuhsin
From *abd* 'servant' + *al-muhsin* 'the benefactor'—in Islam one
of the 100 names of God—
meaning 'servant of the benefactor.'
Alternative spelling: Abdulmohsen.
Famous bearer of the name: Abdulmuhsin ibn Yaqub al-Sahhaf,
poet, born in Bahrain (1874–1931).

## Abdulqadir

From *abd* 'servant' + *al-qadir* 'the powerful'—in Islam one of the 100 names of God—meaning 'servant of the powerful.'
Alternative spelling: Abdulkadir.
Famous bearer of the name: Abdulkadir ibn Muhyi al-Din, Algerian religious and military leader (1808–1883).

## Abdulqawi

From *abd* 'servant' + *al-qawi* 'the powerful'—in Islam one of the 100 names of God—meaning 'servant of the powerful.'
Alternative spelling: Abdulkawi.

## Abdulrahman

From *abd* 'servant' + *al-rahman* 'the merciful'—in Islam one of the 100 names of God—meaning 'servant of the merciful.'
Famous bearer of the name: Abdulrahman I,
first Umayyad emir of Cordoba (died 788).

## Abdulrazzaq

From *abd* 'servant' + *al-razzaq* 'the bestower'—in Islam one of the 100 names of God—meaning 'servant of the bestower.'
Famous bearer of the name: Abdulrazzaq al-Bitar,
Syrian religious and literary scholar (1834–1916).

## Abdulsalam

From *abd* 'servant' + *al-salam* 'peace,'
meaning 'servant of peace.'
Famous bearer of the name: Abdulsalam ibn Abdullah ibn Ziyad, Andalusian-Muslim scholar (died 981).

## Abdulsattar
From *abd* 'servant' + *al-sattar* 'the one who covers sins'—
in Islam one of the 100 names of God—meaning 'servant of
the one who covers sins.'
Famous bearer of the name: Abdulsattar al-Jawari,
Iraqi linguist (1922–1987).

~~~

## Abdulwadud
From *abd* 'servant' + *al-wadud* 'the affectionate'—in Islam
one of the 100 names of God—
meaning 'servant of the affectionate.'

~~~

## Abdulwahhab
From *abd* 'servant' + *al-wahhab* 'the one who gives'—in Islam
one of the 100 names of God—
meaning 'servant of the one who gives.'

~~~

## Abid
Derived from *abd* 'servant.'
Variant: Ubaid.
Famous bearer of the name: Abid ibn al-Abras,
pre-Islamic Arab poet (c. first half of the 6th century).

~~~

## Adham
From *adham* 'very dark.'

## Adib

From *adib* 'educated.'
Famous bearer of the name: Adib Ishaq,
Syrian translator and writer (1857–1885).

∾∾∾

## Adil

From *adil* 'just.'
Alternative spelling: Adel.
Famous bearer of the name: Adil Arslan,
Syrian nationalist and poet (1884–1954).

∾∾∾

## Adnan

From *Adnan*, the legendary ancestor of the Northern Arabs;
a name of pre-Islamic origin.
Famous bearer of the name: Adnan Menderes,
Turkish statesman (1899–1961).

∾∾∾

## Afif

From *afif* 'virtuous.'
Variant: Afifi.
Famous bearer of the name: Afif al-Din al-Talmasani,
Syrian mystic (died 1291).

∾∾∾

## Ahmad

From *ahmad* 'the most praised.'
Alternative spelling: Ahmed.
Famous bearer of the name: Ahmad Shawqi,
Egyptian poet (1868–1932).

### Akram
From *akram* 'very noble' or 'the noblest.'

~~~

### Aladdin
From *ala* 'greatness' + *al-din* 'the religion,'
meaning 'the greatness of religion.'
Famous bearer of the name: Aladdin, the hero of 'Aladdin
and the Wonderful Lamp' in the collection of stories
*Arabian Nights*.

~~~

### Ali
From *ali* 'noble.'
Alternative spelling: Aly.
Famous bearer of the name: Ali ibn Abi Talib,
the fourth caliph (c. 600–661).

~~~

### Amanullah
From *aman* 'protection' + *allah* 'God,'
meaning 'the divine protection.'
Alternative spelling: Amanallah.

~~~

### Amin
From *amin* 'trustworthy.'
Famous bearer of the name: Amin Maalouf,
Lebanese novelist (born 1949).

### Amir

From *amir* 'prince.'
Famous bearer of the name: Amir Khosrow,
Indian writer of Persian language poetry (c. 1253–1325).

### Ammar

From *ammar* 'righteous' or 'steady.'
Famous bearer of the name: Ammar al-Mawsili,
Arab oculist (late 10th/early 11th century).

### Amr

From *amara* 'to live a long time.'
Famous bearer of the name: Amr ibn al-As,
Arab-Muslim military leader and contemporary
of the prophet Muhammad (7th century).

### Anis

From *anis* 'cheerful.'
Variants: Anas, Unais.
Famous bearer of the name: Anis, pen-name of Mir Babar Ali,
Urdu poet of Lucknow, India (1801–1874);
Anis Mansur, Egyptian writer and journalist (born 1924).

### Antar

From *Antar*, famous hero of the Antar epic, considered the
model of the Arabic romance of chivalry.

∿∿∿∿∿∿∿∿∿∿∿∿∿∿

### Anwar
From *anwar* 'lights.'
Alternative spelling: Anouar.
Famous bearer of the name: Anwar al-Sadat,
Egyptian military leader and president (1918–1981);
Anouar Brahem, Tunisian composer (born 1957).

∿∿∿

### Aqil
From *aqil* 'intelligent.'
Alternative spelling: Akil.

∿∿∿

### Arif
From *arif* 'knowing.'
Alternative spelling: Aref.
Famous bearer of the name: Arif ibn Arif al-Muqaddasi,
historian and politician from Palestine (1882–1973).

∿∿∿

### Arslan
From Turkish *arslan* 'lion.'

∿∿∿

### Asad
From *asad* 'lion.'

∿∿∿

### Ashiq
From *ashiq* 'passionate lover.'
Alternative spellings: Asheq, Ashik.
Famous bearer of the name: Ashiq Pasha,
Turkish poet and mystic (1272–1333).

## Ashraf

From *ashraf* 'very honorable' or 'the most honorable.'
Famous bearer of the name: Ashraf Ali Khan,
composer of poetry in Urdu and Persian,
who wrote under the pen-name of Fughan (1727– c. 1773).

❧❧❧

## Asim

From *asim* 'protector.'

❧❧❧

## Atallah

From *ata* 'gift' + *allah* 'God,' meaning 'God's gift.'

❧❧❧

## Atif

From *atif* 'kind.'
Alternative spelling: Atef.
Famous bearer of the name: Atif Sidki,
Egyptian politician and minister (born 1930).

❧❧❧

## Atiq

From *atiq* 'freed slave.'
Alternative spelling: Atik.

❧❧❧

## Ayub

The Arabic form of the biblical Job.
Alternative spelling: Ayoub.

## Aziz

From *aziz* 'powerful' or 'dear.'
Variants: Azzouz, Uzaiz.
Famous bearer of the name: al-Aziz Billah,
fifth Fatimid caliph of Egypt (955–996).

~~~

## Azmi

Derived from  *azm* 'resolution' or 'firm purpose.'
Variant: Azzam.

~~~

# B

## Badhil
From *badhil* 'donor.'
Alternative spellings: Bazil, Bazel.

∾∾∾

## Badr
From *badr* 'full moon.'
Variants: Badir, Bader.
Famous bearer of the name: Badr al-Dib,
Egyptian writer (born 1920).

∾∾∾

## Bahaddin
From *baha* 'splendor' and *al-din* 'the religion,'
meaning 'splendor of the religion.'
Alternative spellings: Bahaëddin, Baha al-Din.
Famous bearer of the name: Baha al-Din Zuhair,
Arab poet of the Ayyubid period (1186–1258).

∾∾∾

## Bahir
From *bahir* 'beautiful' or 'admirable.'
Alternative spelling: Baher.

∾∾∾

## Bakr
From *bakr* 'first-born.'
Variants: Bakir, Abu Bakr.
Famous bearer of the name: Abu Bakr al-Razi (latinized:
Rhazes), physician, alchemist and philosopher (865–925).

### Baligh
From *baligh* 'mature.'
Alternative spelling: Balir.

❧❧❧

### Bashir
From *bashir* 'bearer of good news.'
Variant: Bashar.
Famous bearer of the name: Bashar ibn Burd,
Arab poet (died 783).

❧❧❧

### Basil
From *basil* 'brave.'

❧❧❧

### Bassam
From *bassam* 'smiling.'
Variants: Bassim, Bassem.

❧❧❧

### Bilal
Derived from *ballala* 'to moisten.'
Famous bearer of the name: Bilal ibn Rabah,
the first muezzin of Islam.

❧❧❧

### Bulus
The Arabic form of Paul.

❧❧❧

### Burhan
From *burhan* 'proof.'
Famous bearer of the name: Burhan Karkutli,
Palestinian painter (born 1932).

## Butrus

The Arabic form of Peter.
Alternative spellings: Butros, Boutros.
Famous bearer of the name: Butrus Butrus-Ghali,
United Nations Secretary (born 1922).

# D

## Dalil
From *dalil* 'guide.'

ᑐᑐᑐ

## Dawud
The Arabic form of David.
Alternative spelling: Dawood.
Famous bearer of the name: Dawud al-Fatani,
Malay author (first half of the 19th century).

ᑐᑐᑐ

## Diyaüddin
From *diya* 'light' + *al-din* 'the religion,'
meaning 'light of the religion.'
Alternative spelling: Diyaëddin.

ᑐᑐᑐ

## Diyaülhaqq
From *diya* 'light' + *al-haqq* 'the truth,'
meaning 'light of the truth.'
Alternative spelling: Diyaëlhaqq.

ᑐᑐᑐ

# F

## Fadi
From *fadi* 'someone who sacrifices himself to save others.'

~~~

## Fadil
From *fadil* 'virtuous' or 'excellent.'
Variants: Fudaïl, Fudaïli.
Famous bearer of the name: Fadil Bey,
Ottoman erotic poet (1757–1810).

~~~

## Fahd
From *fahd* 'cheetah.'
Variant: Fahid.
Famous bearer of the name: Fahd ibn Abdulaziz,
king of Saudi Arabia (born 1923).

~~~

## Fahim
From *fahim* 'intelligent' or 'judicious.'
Variant: Fahmi.

~~~

## Faïd
From *faïd* 'abundance.'

~~~

## Faïq
From *faïq* 'excellent' or 'superior.'
Alternative spelling: Faïk.

## Faisal
From *faisal* 'judge' or 'arbiter.'
Alternative spelling: Faysal.
Famous bearers of the name: Faisal ibn Abdulaziz,
king of Saudi Arabia (1905–1975);
Faisal Husseini, Palestinian politician (born 1940).

## Faïz
From *faïz* 'successful' or 'victorious.'
Alternative spelling: Fayez.
Famous bearer of the name: Fayez Khaddur,
Syrian poet (born 1942).

## Farah
From *farah* 'joy'.
Famous bearer of the name: Farah Antun Elias,
Lebanese novelist and journalist (1874–1922).

## Faraj
From *faraj* 'joy' or 'relief.'
Alternative spellings: Farag, Fredj.

## Farhat
From *farhat* 'joy.'
Alternative spelling: Ferhat.
Famous bearer of the name: Ferhat Abbas,
Algerian nationalist leader (1899–1985).

## Farid

From *farid* 'unique' or 'incomparable.'
Famous bearer of the name: Farid al-Atrash,
Egyptian musician of Lebanese origin (1915–1974).

~~~

## Faris

From *faris* 'horseman.'
Alternative spelling: Fares.
Famous bearer of the name: Faris al-Shidyak,
Lebanese writer, lexicographer and poet (1804–1887);
Faris Zarzur, Syrian writer (born 1929).

~~~

## Faruq

From *faruq* 'someone who knows how to distinguish
falsehood from truth.'
Alternative spelling: Faruk.
Famous bearer of the name: Faruq I,
king of Egypt (1920–1965).

~~~

## Fathi

Derived from *fath* 'opening,' meaning 'open-minded.'
Alternative spelling: Fethi.
Famous bearer of the name: Fathi Ghanem,
Egyptian writer and journalist (born 1924).

~~~

## Fathuddin

From *fath* 'victory' or 'conquest' + *al-din* 'the religion,'
meaning 'victory of the religion.'
Alternative spelling: Fatheddin.

### Fatih

From *fatih* 'conqueror' or 'victor.'
Variant: Futaih.

~~~

### Fatim

From *fatim* 'weaned.'

~~~

### Fawz

From *fawz* 'success' or 'escape.'
Variants: Fawzi, Fawaz.
Famous bearer of the name: Fawaz Turki,
Palestinian writer (born 1940);
Fawzi Mellah, Tunisian writer (born 1946).

~~~

### Fayyad

From *fayyad* 'generous.'

~~~

### Fuad

From *fuad* "heart' or 'spirit.'
Alternative spelling: Fouad.
Famous bearer of the name: Fouad I,
King of Egypt (1869–1936).

~~~

# G

## Ghaïth
From *ghaïs* 'abundant rain.'
Alternative spelling: Ghaïs.

ᚾᚾᚾ

## Ghalib
From *ghalib* 'victor.'
Alternative spelling: Ghaleb.
Famous bearer of the name: Ghalib Dede,
Turkish poet (1757–1799).

ᚾᚾᚾ

## Ghani
From *ghani* 'rich' or 'not in need.'

ᚾᚾᚾ

## Ghassan
From *ghasan* 'vigour' or 'fieriness of youth.'
Famous bearer of the name: Ghassan Kanafani,
Palestinian writer (1936–1972).

ᚾᚾᚾ

## Ghazi
From *ghazi* 'warrior' or 'invader.'
Famous bearer of the name: Ghazi, king of Iraq (1912–1939).

ᚾᚾᚾ

# H

## Habib
From *habib* 'beloved.'
Famous bearer of the name: Habib Bourguiba,
first president of Tunisia (born 1903).

≈≈≈

## Habibullah
From *habib* 'beloved' + *allah* 'God,' meaning 'loved by God.'
Alternative spelling: Habiballah.

≈≈≈

## Hadi
From *hadi* 'guide.'
Alternative spelling: Hedi.

≈≈≈

## Hafiz
From *hafiz* 'guardian' or 'keeper.'
Alternative spellings: Hafez, Hafis.
Famous bearer of the name: Hafiz,
Persian poet (c. 1325–1389).

≈≈≈

## Haidar
Derived from *hadara* 'to dwell.'
Alternative spelling: Haider.
Famous bearer of the name: Haidar Abd al-Shafi,
Palestinian politician (born 1919).

### Haitham
From *haitham* 'eagle.'
Alternative spellings: Haisam, Haithem.

~~~

### Hakam
From *hakam* 'arbitrator.'
Famous bearer of the name: Hakam ibn Maïmun al-Wadi,
singer in Baghdad (8th century).

~~~

### Hakim
From *hakim* 'judge.'
Alternative spelling: Hakem, Hakeem.
Famous bearer of the name: Hakeem Olajuwoon,
Nigerian-born basketball player (born 1963).

~~~

### Hamd
From *hamd* 'praise' or 'thanks.'
Variants: Hamdan, Hamdun.
Famous bearer of the name: Hamd Allah-i Mustawfi.
Persian historian, geographer and man of letters (1281–?).

~~~

### Hamid
From *hamid* 'praised.'
Variants: Hamida, Humaid, Hamidi.
Famous bearer of the name: Hamidi,
poet at the court of Mehmet the Conqueror (c. 1427–1485).

~~~

### Hamim
From *hamim* 'close friend.'

### Hammad

From *hammada* 'to praise,' meaning 'someone who fervently praises God' or 'who praises much.'

Variant: Hammadi.

Famous bearer of the name: Hammad al-Rawiya, a collector of Arabic poems, of Iranian origin (c. 694–773).

### Hamza

From *hamza* 'lion.'

Famous bearer of the name: Hamza Fansuri, Indonesian mystic writer (died 1630).

### Hana

From *hana* 'happiness.'

### Hani

From *hani* 'cheerful' or 'happy.'

Famous bearer of the name: Hani al-Rahib, Syrian writer (born 1939).

### Hanif

From *hanif* 'having the right belief.'

Variant: Hanifa.

### Haris

From *haris* 'watchman' or 'guard.'

### Harun

The Arabic form of Aaron.
Alternative spelling: Haroun.
Famous bearer of the name: Harun al-Rashid,
Abbasid caliph (766–809).

~~~

### Hashim

From *hashim* 'generous' or bountiful.'
Alternative spelling: Hashem.

~~~

### Hasib

From *hasib* 'noble' or 'venerated.'

~~~

### Hassan

From *hasan* 'excellent' or 'handsome.'
Famous bearer of the name: Hassan II,
king of Morroco (born 1929).

~~~

### Hassun

From *hassun* 'goldfinch.'
Alternative spelling: Hassoun.

~~~

### Hatif

From *hatif*, meaning 'leader of a ceremony
of a mystical religious order.'
Famous bearer of the name: Hatif of Isfahan,
Persian poet (died c. 781).

### Hatim

Derived from *hatama* 'to decide' or 'to decree.'
Alternative spelling: Hatem.
Famous bearer of the name: Hatem al-Makki,
Tunisian painter (born 1918).

### Hisham

From *hisham* 'bounty' or 'generosity.'
Famous bearer of the name: Hisham III,
the last of the Umayyad caliphs of Cordoba (c. 975–1036).

### Husam

From *husam* 'sword.'
Variant: Hasam.
Famous bearer of the name: Husam al-Khatib,
Palestinian literary critic (born 1932).

### Husni

From *husn* 'beauty.'
Alternative spellings: Housni, Hosni.
Famous bearer of the name: Hosni Mubarak,
president of Egypt (born 1928).

### Hussain

Diminutive of the name Hassan.
Alternative spellings: Hussein, Huseyn.
Famous bearer of the name: Hussein,
king of Jordan (born 1935).

# I

## Ibrahim
The Arabic form of Abraham.
Alternative spelling: Ebrahim.
Variant: Brahim.
Famous bearer of the name: Ibrahim Tuqan,
Palestinian poet (1905–1941).

~~~

## Idris
From *idris* 'studious person.'
Famous bearer of the name: Idris I,
king of Libya (1890–1983).

~~~

## Ihsan
From *ihsan* 'beneficence.'
Famous bearer of the name: Ihsan Abd al-Quddus,
Egyptian journalist and writer (1918–1990).

~~~

## Ilyas
The Arabic form of the prophet Elijah,
meaning 'Jehovah is God.'
Alternative spelling: Elias.
Famous bearer of the name: Elias Khoury,
Lebanese writer (born 1948).

~~~

## Imad
From *imad* 'pillar.'
Alternative spelling: Emad.

## Imaduddin

From *imad* 'pillar' + *al-din* 'the religion,'
meaning 'pillar of the religion.'
Famous bearer of the name: Imaduddin al-Isfahani,
Persian historian (1125–1201).

~~~

## Imadullah

From *imad* 'pillar' + *allah* 'God,' meaning 'pillar of God.'
Alternative spelling: Imadallah.

~~~

## Imran

The Arabic form of the Hebrew name Amram.
Variants: Amran, Umran.

~~~

## Iqbal

From *iqbal* 'prosperity.'
Alternative spellings: Iqbal, Ekbal.

~~~

## Irfan

Derived from *irfan* 'recognition.'

~~~

## Isa

The Arabic form Jesus.
Alternative spellings: Issa, Esa.
Famous bearer of the name: Issa Naouri, Jordanian writer
(born 1918); Issa Bullata, Palestinian critic (born 1929).

## Isam

From *isam* 'strap' or 'tie.'

~~~

## Ishaq

The Arabic form of Isaac.
Alternative spelling: Ishak.

~~~

## Iskandar

The Arabic form of the Greek name Alexander.
Famous bearer of the name: Iskandar Antun,
Lebanese legist and literate (1875–1920).

~~~

## Ismaïl

The Arabic form of Ishmael, son of Abraham.
Famous bearer of the name: Ismaïl Merchant,
film director and producer (born 1936).

~~~

## Iyad

From *ayyada* 'to support' or 'to strengthen.'

~~~

## Izzuddin

From *izz* 'mightiness' + *al-din* 'the religion,'
meaning 'mightiness of the religion.'
Variant: Azzedin.
Famous bearer of the name: Izzuddin ibn al-Athir,
Arab chronicler (1160–1233).

~~~

# J

## Jabir
From *jabara* 'to console' or 'to comfort.'
Alternative spelling: Jaber.
Famous bearer of the name: Jabir ibn Hayyan,
Arabian alchemist of Khorasan origin (c. 721–815).

~~~

## Jabr
Diminutive of *jabr* 'power' or 'might.'
Variant: Jubaïr.

~~~

## Jafar
From *jafar* 'stream' or 'brook.'
Famous bearer of the name: Jafar al-Sadiq,
the last imam recognized by both Twelver Shiites and
Ismaïlites (c. 699–765).

~~~

## Jahid
Derived from *jahada* 'to make an effort' or 'to exert oneself.'
Alternative spelling: Jahed.

~~~

## Jalal
From *jalal* 'splendor' or 'majesty.'
Alternative spelling: Galal.
Famous bearer of the name: Jalal Ben Abdallah,
Tunisian painter (born 1921).

## Jalaluddin

From *jalal* 'splendor' or 'majesty' + *al-din* 'the religion,'
meaning 'splendor of the religion.'
Alternative spelling: Jalaleddin.
Famous bearer of the name: Jalal al-Din Muhammad Rumi,
Persian poet and mystic (1207–1273).

~~~

## Jalil

From *jalil* 'great.'

~~~

## Jamal

From *jamal* 'beauty' or 'grace.'
Alternative spelling: Gamal.
Famous bearer of the name: Gamal Abdel Nasser,
Egyptian officer and statesman (1918–1970);
Gamal al-Ghitani, Egyptian novelist (born 1945).

~~~

## Jamaluddin

From *jamal* 'beauty' or 'grace' + *al-din* 'the religion,'
meaning 'grace of the religion.'
Alternative spellings: Jamaleddin, Gamaleddin.
Famous bearer of the name: Jamaluddin al-Afghani,
Islamic theorist (c. 1838–1897).

~~~

## Jamil

From *jamil* 'handsome.'
Variant: Gamil.

## Jawad

From *jawad* 'generous.'
Famous bearer of the name: Jawad Pasha,
Ottoman minister and writer (1851–1900).

~~~

## Jubran

Derived from *jabr* 'power' or 'might.'
Variants: Jibran, Gibran.
Famous bearer of the name: Jibran Khalil Jibran,
Lebanese-American writer and poet (1883–1931).

~~~

## Jund

From *janada* 'soldiers' or 'army.'
Variants: Junaïd, Junaïdi.

~~~

## Jurji

The Arabic form of George.
Famous bearer of the name: Jurji Zaidan,
Lebanese historian and writer (1861–1914).

~~~

# K

## Kaab

From *kaab* 'fame' or glory.'
Famous bearer of the name: Kaab ibn Zuhair,
Arabic poet (first half of the 7th century).

### Kafil

From *kafil* 'guarantor.'

### Kamal

From *kamal* 'perfection.'
Variants: Kamil, Kumail.
Famous bearer of the name: Kamal Nasir,
Palestinian poet (1925–1973).

### Kamaluddin

From *kamal* 'perfection' + *al-din* 'the religion,'
meaning 'perfection of the religion.'
Alternative spelling: Kamaleddin.

### Karim

From *karim* 'noble' or 'liberal.'
Alternative spellings: Kerim, Kareem.
Variant: Kuraim.
Famous bearer of the name: Kareem Abdul Jabbar,
American basketball player (born 1947).

### Khalid

From *khalid* 'everlasting.'
Alternative spelling: Khaled.
Variant: Khaldun.
Famous bearer of the name: Khalid ibn al-Walid,
Arab commander (died 642).

## Khalil

From *khalil* 'friend.'
Famous bearer of the name: Khalil Mutran,
Lebanese poet (1872–1949).

~~~

## Khalis

From *khalis* 'pure.'
Alternative spelling: Khales.

~~~

# L

## Labib

From *labib* 'intelligent.'
Variant: Lubaib.
Famous bearer of the name: Labib al-Riashi,
Lebanese journalist and literate (1889–1966).

~~~

## Lutf

From *lutf* 'friendliness.'
Variants: Lutfi, Lotfi.
Famous bearer of the name: Lutfi al-Khuli,
Egyptian short story writer and playwright (born 1928).

~~~

## Lutfullah

From *lutf* 'friendliness' + *allah* 'God,'
meaning 'God's friendliness.'
Alternative spellings: Lutfallah, Lotfallah.

~~~

# M

### Maamar
Derived from *amara* 'to live a long time.'
Variant: Muammar.

~~~

### Maamun
From *maamun* 'trustworthy.'
Alternative spellings: Maamoun, Mamun.
Famous bearer of the name: al-Maamun, seventh Abbasid
caliph and eldest son of Harun al-Rashid (786–833).

~~~

### Maaruf
From *maaruf* 'kindness.'
Alternative spelling: Maarouf.
Famous bearer of the name: Maruf al-Rusafi,
Iraqi poet (1875–1945).

~~~

### Mabruk
From *mabruk* 'blessed.'
Alternative spelling: Mabrouk.

~~~

### Madih
From *madih* 'one who eulogizes.'

~~~

### Mahbub
From *mahbub* 'beloved' or 'liked.'
Alternative spelling: Mahboub.
Famous bearer of the name: Mahbub ibn al-Rahil Abu Sufyan,
theologian and historian (8th century).

## Mahdi

From *mahdi* 'rightly guided.'
Alternative spelling: Mehdi.

~~~

## Mahfuz

From *mahfuz* 'guarded' or 'preserved.'
Alternative spelling: Mahfouz.

~~~

## Mahir

From *mahir* 'skilful.'
Alternative spelling: Maher.

~~~

## Mahmud

From *mahmud* 'praised' or 'praiseworthy.'
Alternative spellings: Mahmoud, Mahmood.
Famous bearer of the name: Mahmud Darwish,
Palestinian poet and writer (born 1941).

~~~

## Majdi

From *majdi* 'glorious.'
Alternative spellings: Magdi, Mejdi.
Famous bearer of the name: Majdi al-Aqili,
Syrian musician (1917–1984).

~~~

## Majduddin

From *majd* 'glory' or 'praise' and *al-din* 'religion,'
meaning 'glory of religion.'
Alternative spelling: Majdeddin.

### Majid
From *majid* 'noble' or 'glorious.'
Famous bearer of the name: Majid ibn Saïd,
sultan of Zanzibar (1835–1870).

~~~

### Makin
From *makin* 'strong.'

~~~

### Malih
Derived from *malah* 'to be beautiful.'

~~~

### Malik
From *malik* 'king.'
Alternative spelling: Malek.
Famous bearer of the name: Malik ibn Abi al-Samh,
Arab folklorist musician (died 754); Malik Haddad,
Algerian literate and poet (1927–1978).

~~~

### Mamduh
From *mamduh* 'praised.'

~~~

### Mansur
From *mansur* 'aided by God' or 'victorious.'
Alternative spellings: Mansour, Mansoor.
Famous bearer of the name: Mansur, painter of miniatures
during the Mughal period in India (16th/17th century).

~~~

### Maqbul
From *maqbul* 'accepted.'
Alternative spelling: Makbul.

### Marwan
Derived from *marw* 'pebble' or 'flint.'
Famous bearer of the name: Marwan II,
last of the Umayyad caliphs of Syria (died 750).

~~~

### Marzuq
From *marzuq* 'blessed with worldly goods.'

~~~

### Masud
From *masud* 'favored by luck' or 'lucky.'
Alternative spelling: Masoud.

~~~

### Mawhub
From *mawhub* 'talented' or 'gifted.'
Alternative spelling: Mawhoub.

~~~

### Mawlud
From *mawlud* 'newly born.'
Alternative spelling: Mawloud.

~~~

### Muayyad
From *muayyad* 'helped' or 'supported.'
Famous bearer of the name: al-Muayyad bi-llah Muhammad,
imam of Yemen (1582–1644).

~~~

### Mubarak
From *mubarak* 'blessed.'
Alternative spelling: Moubarak.
Famous bearer of the name: Mubarak Rabi,
Moroccan writer (born 1935).

### Mubashir

From *mubashir* 'someone who brings good news.'
Famous bearer of the name: al-Mubashir ibn Fatik,
Egyptian historian and savant (11th century).

### Mufid

From *mufid* 'beneficial.'
Alternative spelling: Moufid.

### Muhammad

From *muhammad* 'highly praised.'
Alternative spellings: Mohammed, Mohamed.
Famous bearers of the name: Muhammad Abdulwahhab,
Egyptian singer and composer (1910–1991); Muhammad Ali,
American boxer (born 1942).

### Muhibb

From *muhib* 'venerable' or 'dignified.'
Alternative spelling: Moheb.
Famous bearer of the name: Muhibb Ahmed Diranas,
Turkish poet and dramatist (1909–1980).

### Muhiüddin

From *muhin* 'one who inspires' + *al-din* 'religion,' meaning
'one who inspires the religion.'
Alternative spelling: Mouhyeddin.
Famous bearer of the name: Muhiüddin ibn al-Arabi,
Arab mystical writer (1165–1240).

### Muhsin
From *muhsin* 'benefactor.'
Alternative spelling: Mohsen.
Famous bearer of the name: Muhsin-i Fayd-i Qashani,
scholar in Safawid Persia (1598–1679).

~~~

### Muhtadi
From *muhtadi* 'rightly guided.'
Alternative spelling: Mohtadi.
Famous bearer of the name: al-Muhtadi bi-llah,
Abbasid caliph (died 870).

~~~

### Mujahid
From *mujahid* 'fighter.'

~~~

### Mukhlis
From *mukhlis* 'sincere.'

~~~

### Mukhtar
From *mukhtar* 'preferred' or 'chosen (by God).'
Alternative spelling: Mokhtar.
Famous bearer of the name: Mukhtar al-Wakil,
Egyptian poet and critic (1911–1988).

~~~

### Mumin
From *mumin* 'believer.'
Variant: Moumin.

### Mundhir
From *mundhir* 'one who warns.'
Alternative spellings: Munzir, Mondher, Munther.
Famous bearer of the name: al-Mundhir ibn Muhammad,
sixth Umayyad amir of Cordoba (844–888).

∾∾∾

### Munib
From *munib* 'repentant.'
Alternative spelling: Mounib.

∾∾∾

### Munif
From *munif* 'sublime' or 'excellent.'
Alternative spelling: Mounif.

∾∾∾

### Munir
From *munir* 'luminous' or 'shining.'
Alternative spelling: Mounir.
Famous bearer of the name: Munir Salih Abd al-Qadir,
Sudanese poet (died 1991).

∾∾∾

### Munji
Derived from *naja* 'to escape.'
Alternative spelling: Monji.

∾∾∾

### Munsif
From *munsif* 'someone who thinks justly and fairly.'
Alternative spellings: Monsef, Moncef.
Famous bearer of the name: Moncef Ghachem,
Tunisian writer (born 1946).

### Muntasir
From *muntasir* 'victorious' or 'conquering.'
Alternative spelling: Montaser.

### Muqbil
From *muqbil* 'someone who approaches.'

### Murad
From *murad* 'desired.'
Alternative spellings: Mourad, Morad.
Famous bearer of the name: Murad I,
Ottoman sultan (died 1389).

### Murid
From *murid* 'disciple' or 'novice.'

### Murtadha
Derived from *irtadha* 'to be content with.'

### Musa
The Arabic form of Moses.
Famous bearer of the name: Musa Sabri,
Egyptian writer (1925–1992).

### Musaddaq
From *musaddaq* 'sincere' or 'trustworthy.'
Alternative spelling: Mosaddak.

## Mustafa
From *mustafa* 'selected.'
Alternative spellings: Mostafa, Mustapha, Mostapha.
Famous bearer of the name: Mustafa Kamal,
Egyptian nationalist leader (1874–1908).

~~~

## Mutasim
From *mutasim* 'someone who takes refuge.'
Alternative spellings: Moutasim, Moutasem.

~~~

## Mutawakkil
Derived from *tawakkala* 'to trust in someone' or
'to be nominated as a deputy.'
Famous bearer of the name: Mutawakkil ibn Abi Hussein,
Andalusian poet (11th century).

~~~

## Muzaffar
From *muzaffar* 'victorious' or 'conqueror.'
Alternative spelling: Mozaffar.
Famous bearer of the name: Muzaffar Shams Balkhi,
medieval Indian Sufi master (c. 1320–1400).

~~~

### Nabih
From *nabih* 'noble' or 'excellent.'

~~~

### Nabil
From *nabil* 'noble' or 'aristocratic.'
Famous bearer of the name: Nabil al-Selmi,
Egyptian artist and caricaturist (1941–1987).

~~~

### Nadhir
From *nadhir* 'dedicated to God.'
Alternative spellings: Nazir, Nazer.
Famous bearer of the name: Nadhir Ahmad Dihlawi,
Urdu prose writer (1836–1912).

~~~

### Nadim
From *nadim* 'associate' or 'friend.'
Famous bearer of the name: Nadim al-Darwish,
Syrian musician (1926–1987).

~~~

### Nadir
From *nadir* 'rare' or 'precious.'
Alternative spelling: Nader.
Famous bearer of the name: Nadir Shah Afshar,
Turkmen ruler (1688–1747).

~~~

### Nafis
From *nafis* 'valuable' or 'precious.'

## Naïm
From *naïm* 'contended' or 'tranquil.'

~~~

## Naïmullah
From *naïm* 'gift of grace' + *allah* 'God,'
meaning 'gift given by God.'
Alternative spelling: Naïmallah.

~~~

## Naji
From *naji* 'close friend.'
Alternative spelling: Nagi.

~~~

## Najib
From *najib* 'noble.'
Alternative spellings: Najeeb, Naguib.
Famous bearer of the name: Naguib Mahfouz,
Egyptian writer and winner of the Nobel prize
for literature (born 1911).

~~~

## Najid
Derived from *najada* 'to help' or 'to aid.'

~~~

## Najmuddin
From *najm* 'star' + *al-din* 'the religion,'
meaning 'star of the religion.'
Alternative spelling: Najmeddin.

## Nashit

From *nashit* 'active' or 'energetic.'
Famous bearer of the name: Nashit, singer of Persian origin and former slave, in Medina (7th century).

~~~

## Nasir

From *nasir* 'helper.'
Alternative spelling: Nasser.
Famous bearer of the name: Nasir-i Khusraw,
Persian poet and prose writer (1004–1072).

~~~

## Nasr

From *nasr* 'help' or 'victory.'
Variant: Nasri.

~~~

## Nayyir

From *nayyir* 'shining' or 'bright.'

~~~

## Nazim

From *nazim* 'poet.'
Famous bearer of the name: Nazim Hikmet,
Turkish poet (1902–1963).

~~~

## Nidal

From *nidal* 'combat.'

~~~

## Nima

From *nima* 'blessing.'

### Nizam
From *nizam* 'order.'
Famous bearer of the name: Nizam al-Mulk,
minister of the Saljukid sultans (died 1092).

～～～

### Nizar
From *nazara* 'to decide' or 'to consider.'
Famous bearer of the name: Nizar Qabbani,
Syrian poet and writer (born 1923).

～～～

### Numan
From *numan* 'blood.'
Alternative spelling: Naaman.
Famous bearer of the name: Numan Ashour,
Egyptian playwright (1918–1987).

～～～

### Nuri
From *nuri* 'brilliant' or 'bright.'
Alternative spelling: Nouri.
Famous bearer of the name: Nuri al-Said,
Iraqi politician (1888–1958).

～～～

### Nuruddin
From *nur* 'light' + *al-din* 'the religion,'
meaning 'the light of religion.'
Alternative spellings: Nureddin, Noureddin.
Famous bearer of the name: Nuruddin Jami,
Persian poet, mystic and scholar (1414–1492);
Noureddin Muhammed, Tunisian writer (1914–1990).

## Q

### Qasim

Derived from *qasam* 'beauty' or 'elegance.'
Alternative spelling: Kassem.
Famous bearer of the name: Qassim Amin, Egyptian writer
and social thinker (1863–1908).

~~~

### Qayim

From *qayim* 'straight' or 'true.'
Alternative spelling: Kayim.

~~~

## R

### Rafiq

From *rafiq* 'companion.'
Alternative spelling: Rafik.
Famous bearer of the name: Rafiq al-Hariri,
Lebanese prime minister (born 1944).

~~~

### Rahim

From *rahim* 'compassionate.'

~~~

### Raïd

From *raïd* 'champion' or 'pioneer.'
Alternative spelling: Raed.
Variant: Ruwaid.

### Raji
From *raji* 'hopeful.'

ᖇᖇᖇ

### Ramin
From *ramin* 'archer.'

ᖇᖇᖇ

### Ramis
From *ramasa* 'to cover.'
Variant: Rumais.

ᖇᖇᖇ

### Ramzi
From *ramzi* 'symbolic.'
Famous bearer of the name: Ramzi Nagui,
Egyptian musician (born 1948).

ᖇᖇᖇ

### Raouf
From *raouf* 'compassionate.'
Famous bearer of the name: Raouf Abdulmajid Hamza,
Egyptian painter (born 1932).

ᖇᖇᖇ

### Rashad
From *rashad* 'rightness of action.'

ᖇᖇᖇ

### Rashid
From *rashid* 'follower of the right way.'
Alternative spellings: Rachid, Rasheed.
Famous bearer of the name: Rashid Rida, Islamic reformer
(1885–1935); Rachid Boujedra, Algerian writer (born 1941).

## Razi
From *radi* 'satisfied' or 'content.'

### Riad
From *riad* 'meadows.'
Alternative spelling: Riyad.
Famous bearer of the name: Riyad al-Sulh,
Lebanese nationalist and politician (1894–1951).

### Rida
From *rida* 'satisfaction.'
Alternative spellings: Ridha, Redha, Reza.

### Ridwan
From *ridwan* 'satisfaction.'
Variant: Radwan.

### Rizq
From *rizq* 'means of living.'

### Ruhi
From *ruhi* 'spiritual.'
Alternative spelling: Rouhi.

### Rushd
From *rushd* 'rectitude' or 'maturity.'
Alternative spelling: Roshd.
Variants: Rushdi, Rushdan.
Famous bearer of the name: Ibn Rushd,
Andalusian philisopher (1126–1198).

### Saad
From *saad* 'luck' or 'success.'
Variant: Saadi.
Famous bearer of the name: Saad Zaghloul,
Egyptian jurist and politician (1858–1927).

### Sabih
From *sabih* 'handsome.'

### Sabir
From *sabir* 'patient.'
Alternative spelling: Saber.
Famous bearer of the name: Sabir ibn Ismaïl al-Tirmidhi
Shihab al-Din, known as Adib Sabir,
Persian poet (first half of the 12th century).

### Sabri
From *sabr* 'patience.'

### Sadid
From *sadid* 'right' or 'true.'

### Sadiq
From *sadiq* 'friend.'
Alternative spellings: Sadik, Sadek.
Famous bearer of the name: Sadiq Hedayat,
Persian writer (1903–1951).

## Sahib
From *sahib* 'companion.'

~~~

## Saïd
From *saïd* 'fortunate' or 'happy.'
Alternative spelling: Saeed.
Famous bearer of the name: Saïd Aql,
Lebanese poet (born 1912).

~~~

## Sajid
From *sajid* 'worshipper.'
Alternative spelling: Sajed.

~~~

## Sajjad
From *sajjad* 'pious worshipper.'

~~~

## Salah
From *salah* 'goodness' or 'virtue.'
Famous bearer of the name: Salah Abd al-Sabur,
Egyptian poet and playwright (1931–1958).

~~~

## Salahuddin
From *salah* 'virtue' + *al-din* 'the religion,'
meaning 'virtue of religion.'
Alternative spellings: Salaheddin, Saladin.
Famous bearer of the name: Salah al-Din Yusuf,
military leader of Kurdish origin who recaptured Jerusalem
from the Crusaders (1138–1193).

### Salama
From *salama* 'faultlessness.'
Famous bearer of the name: Salama Musa,
Egyptian encyclopedist and journalist (c. 1887–1958).

### Salih
From *salih* 'good' or 'just.'
Alternative spelling: Saleh.

### Salim
From *salim* 'faultless.'
Alternative spelling: Saleem, Slim, Selim.
Famous bearer of the name: Salim Barakat,
Syrian writer (born 1951).

### Salman
From *salima* 'to be sound, safe.'
Famous bearer of the name: Salman Rushdie,
British novelist of Indian descent (born 1947).

### Sami
From *sami* 'high' or 'noble.'

### Samih
From *samih* 'lenient' or 'tolerant.'

### Samir
From *samir* 'entertainer' or 'narrator.'

## Sayid

From *sayid* 'master' or 'lord.'
Alternative spelling: Sayed.

~~~

## Shadi

From *shadi* 'educated.'

~~~

## Shafi

From *shafi* 'curing' or 'healing.'

~~~

## Shafiq

From *shafiq* 'compassionate.'
Famous bearer of the name: Shafiq Shamiya,
Egyptian film producer (born 1934).

~~~

## Shahid

From *shahid* 'witness' or 'martyr.'
Variant: Shuhaid.
Famous bearer of the name: Shahid,
philosopher and poet in Persian and Arabic (died 927).

~~~

## Shakib

From Persian, meaning 'patience' or 'steadiness.'
Alternative spelling: Shekib.
Famous bearer of the name: Shakib Arslan,
Syrian writer and poet (1869–1946).

### Shakir
From *shakir* 'thankful.'
Alternative spelling: Shaker.
Famous bearer of the name: Shakir Faïk al-Nabulsi,
Jordanian writer (born 1940).

~~~

### Sharif
From *sharif* 'honorable.'
Alternative spelling: Sherif.

~~~

### Shawqi
From *shawq* 'strong desire.'
Famous bearer of the name: Shawqi Baghdadi,
Syrian writer (born 1928).

~~~

### Shihab
From *shihab* 'meteor.'

~~~

### Shukri
From *shukri* 'thanking.'

~~~

### Sidqi
Derived from *sidq* 'truth' or 'sincerity.'
Alternative spelling: Sedki.

~~~

### Sirajuddin
From *siraj* 'light' + *al-din* 'the religion,'
meaning 'light of the religion.'
Alternative spelling: Sirajeddin.

## Sufian
Derived from *safa* 'to raise and scatter dust' (said of the wind).
Alternative spelling: Sofian.
Famous bearer of the name: Sufian al-Abdi,
Arab poet in Kufa (8th century).

～～～

## Suhaib
Derived from *sahiba* 'to be friends with someone.'

～～～

## Suhail
From *suhail* 'canopus', a star of the first magnitude in the
constellation Carina.'
Alternative spelling: Souheil.

## Sulaiman
The Arabic form Solomon.
Alternative spelling: Soleiman, Sulaima.
Famous bearer of the name: Sulaiman,
tenth Ottoman sultan (c. 1494–1566).

～～～

# T

## Taha

Name formed from the combination of the letters *t* and *h* at the beginning of the 20th sura of the Koran.
Famous bearer of the name: Taha Hussein,
Egyptian writer (1889–1973).

## Tahir

From *tahir* 'pure' or 'innocent.'
Alternative spelling: Taher.

## Taieb

From *taieb* 'good.'
Alternative spellings: Tayib, Tayeb.

## Taïmullah

Derived from *tama* 'to be devoted' + *allah* 'God,'
meaning 'someone who is devoted to God.'
Alternative spelling: Taïmallah.

## Tajuddin

From *taj* 'crown' + *al-din* 'the religion,'
meaning 'crown of the religion.'
Alternative spelling: Tajeddin.

## Takiüddin

From *taki* 'devout' + *al-din* 'the religion,'
meaning 'a religious, devout person.'
Alternative spelling: Takiëddin.

### Talal

Derived from *tall* 'finest rain' or 'dew.'
Famous bearer of the name: Talal ibn Abdullah,
king of Jordan (1911–1972).

### Talib

From *talib* 'seeker.'
Alternative spelling: Taleb.

### Tamim

Derived from *tamma* 'to be complete.'

### Tariq

From *tariq* 'night visitor.'
Alternative spellings: Tarik, Tarek.
Famous bearer of the name: Tariq ibn Ziyad,
Muslim general who invaded Spain (680–720).

### Tawfiq

From *tawfiq* 'success' or 'prosperity.'
Alternative spelling: Tawfik.
Famous bearer of the name: Tawfiq al-Hakim,
Egyptian playwright and novelist (c. 1898–1987).

### Tharwat

From *tharwa* 'wealth' or 'riches.'

# U

### Umar
From *amara* 'to live a long time.'
Alternative spelling: Omar.
Famous bearers of the name: Omar Khayyam (c. 1050–1122),
Persian poet; Omar Sharif, Egyptian actor (born 1932).

❧❧❧

### Uqba
From *ukba* 'end' or 'issue.'
Alternative spelling: Okba.
Famous bearer of the name: Oqba ibn Nafi,
Arab military leader (died 683).

❧❧❧

### Usaid
Diminutive of *asad* 'lion.'

❧❧❧

### Usama
From *usama* 'lion.'
Alternative spelling: Osama.

❧❧❧

### Uthman
From *uthman* 'young snake.'
Alternative spellings: Othman, Osman.
Famous bearer of the name: Uthman ibn Affan,
third caliph of Islam (died 656); Osman, founder of the
Ottoman dynasty (1258–1324).

❧❧❧

### Uwais
Diminutive of *aïs* 'night wanderer.'

# W

**Wadi**
From *wadi* 'gentle.'

~~~

**Wadid**
From *wadid* 'affectionate.'

~~~

**Wafiq**
Derived from *wafaqa* 'to agree.'
Alternative spelling: Wafik.

~~~

**Wahib**
From *wahib* 'donator.'

~~~

**Wahid**
From *wahid* 'unique.'

~~~

**Waïl**
From *waïl* 'someone who takes refuge.'
Alternative spelling: Wael.

~~~

**Wajdi**
Derived from *wajd* 'passion.'

~~~

**Wajid**
From *wajid* 'enamored.'

## Wajih
From *wajih* 'chief' or 'prince.'

≈≈≈

## Wakil
From *wakil* 'deputy.'

≈≈≈

## Wali
From *wali* 'master' or 'lord.'

≈≈≈

## Walid
From *walid* 'newborn.'

≈≈≈

## Wasil
From *wasil* 'inseparable friend' or 'intimate.'

≈≈≈

## Wasim
From *wasim* 'good looking' or 'handsome.'

≈≈≈

# Ụ

## Yahya
Derived from *hayya* 'to grant someone a long life.'
Famous bearer of the name: Yahya Turki,
Tunisian painter (1901–1969);
Yahya Haqqi, Egyptian writer and critic (1905–1992).

## Yaqub
The Arabic form of Jacob.
Alternative spelling: Yakub.
Famous bearer of the name: Yaqub Yusuf al-Sabee,
Kuwaiti poet (born 1947).

## Yaqzan
From *yaqzan* 'watchful' or 'vigilant.'

## Yasir
From *yasir* 'wealthy.'
Alternative spellings: Yassir, Yasser.
Famous bearer of the name: Yasir Arafat,
Palestinian statesman (born 1929).

## Yassin
Name formed from the combination of the letters *y* and *s*,
invoking a blessing at the beginning of a sura from the Koran.
Famous bearer of the name: Kateb Yassin (originally:
Yassin Kateb), Algerian novelist (1929–1990).

## Yuhanna

The Arabic form of John.

~~~

## Yumni

Derived from *yumn* 'success' or 'luck.'

~~~

## Yunus

The Arabic form of Jonah.

~~~

## Yusr

From *yusr* 'wealth.'
Variant: Yusri.

~~~

## Yusuf

The Arabic form of Joseph.
Alternative spellings: Yusef, Yousef.
Famous bearer of the name: Yusuf Idris,
Egyptian writer and playwright (1927–1991);
Yusuf Islam (orginally: Cat Stevens),
American singer (born 1948).

~~~

# Z

## Zafar
From *zafar* 'victory.'

~~~

## Zafir
From *zafir* 'victorious.'

~~~

## Zahid
From *zahid* 'ascetic.'
Alternative spelling: Zahed.

~~~

## Zahir
From *zahir* 'radiant.'
Alternative spelling: Zaher.

~~~

## Zaïd
Derived from *zada* 'to grow.'
Alternative spellings: Zeid.
Variants: Ziyad, Ziad.
Famous bearer of the name: Zaid Mutiy Dammaj,
Yemenite writer (born 1943).

~~~

## Zaïm
From *zaïm* 'chief' or 'spokesman.'

~~~

## Zain
From *zain* 'embellishment.'
Alternative spelling: Zein.

### Zakariya
The Arabic form of Zacharias/Zachary.
Alternative spelling: Zakariyya.

### Zaki
From *zaki* 'pure' or 'innocent.'
Alternative spelling: Zaky.